I0424118

The Pith of Life: Aphorisms in Honor of Liberty

JAKUB BOŻYDAR WIŚNIEWSKI

Published 2015 by Jakub Bożydar Wiśniewski.

ISBN: 1515335100
ISBN-13: 978-1515335108

CONTENTS

Preface   1

Entrepreneurship, Business, Economics, and Politics   4

Liberty, Authority, and Power   15

Money, Greed, Equality, Envy, and Charity   34

Comfort, Distress, Happiness, and Trouble   41

Aesthetics, Culture, and Taste   44

Knowledge, Expectations, Order, and Chaos   47

PREFACE

Liberty is the central element of human nature. It is the essence of will, the source of creativity, and a prerequisite of virtue. As such, it is also the driving force of civilization and the foundation of any working society. And yet, being an abstract concept, its precise nature is often inadequately understood. This is unfortunate, since, while liberty can work its miracles when used by those who understand it only on an intuitive level, it remains fragile until it is comprehended on a deeper, philosophical level as well.

Luckily, there exists a substantial literature whose aim is to promote this second, more robust kind of understanding. The present book aspires to contribute to the literature in question, especially to this branch of it, represented by names such as Frederic Bastiat, H. L. Mencken, and Henry Hazlitt, that puts particular emphasis on the pithiness and lucidity of the conveyed message. This is where the form of aphorism, with its motto of maximum content in minimum space, becomes particularly useful, especially given the information age's healthy preference for brevity. The beauty of an aphorism is that it does not have to sacrifice brevity for depth, just as liberty does not have to sacrifice efficiency for equity: their best features reinforce one another rather than being opposed. Perhaps in this sense liberty is the most aphoristic of human qualities and the aphorism is the most libertarian of literary forms.

The following collection of aphorisms is grouped into six sets of topics, all related to the overarching topic of liberty and useful in highlighting its various facets. Such an arrangement is based on my belief that the elusive nature of liberty and its unique significance can be fully appreciated only by investigating the concept in question from a variety of perspectives.

The first set is centered on the topics of economics and entrepreneurship. Economics is a sound understanding of the logic of human action, while entrepreneurship is a sound application of the logic of

1

human action. In other words, economics explains the impassable limits imposed upon human liberty by the ineradicable scarcity of resources, while entrepreneurship demonstrates the scope of productive activities and beneficial goals that can be accomplished within those limits. Thus, economics explains the logical relationship between liberty and prosperity, while entrepreneurship demonstrates how to make the most of it. Both topics have to be properly understood if one is to properly appreciate the blessings of liberty: that is, benefit from the endless wealth of opportunities that it offers without at the same time expecting it to deliver the impossible.

The second set deals with the relationship between liberty and its main enemies: authority and power. All human beings are equal in liberty, and thus no individual has the right to use his liberty to curtail the liberty of others, nor can he delegate such a right to anyone else. And yet, there exists a widespread belief that such a delegation is permissible and even beneficial. This belief is the foundation and lifeblood of what is commonly known as politics. By dividing humankind into rulers and ruled, the phenomenon of politics reveals itself as clearly incompatible with the aforementioned principle of equality of liberty, which hints at its essentially destructive and corrupting nature. A thorough understanding of this nature is needed if the phenomenon in question is to be successfully rejected as an antiquated, uncivilized, and highly pernicious form of decision making, and subsequently replaced by peaceful, voluntary, and contractual alternatives.

The third set deals with the topics of money, greed, equality, envy, and charity. Sound money is both the offspring and the vehicle of liberty. It facilitates trade, allows for economic calculation, and serves as a hedge against the uncertain future. And yet, just as in the case of liberty, its relatively abstract nature often makes people insufficiently appreciative of its benefits. This lack of appreciation is particularly dangerous when it is motivated and reinforced by the vices of greed and envy. These, in turn, are often rationalized as a desire for material equality, but while certain kinds of equality are necessary to enjoy the advantages of monetary exchange, the kind referred to here is not to be found among them. This is why it is crucial to make the relevant conceptual distinctions, and aphoristic pithiness may turn out to be particularly helpful in this context. It may also help illuminate the relationship between moneymaking and charitable giving, which is at the heart of the much misunderstood issue of efficiency and equity.

The fourth set is focused on the concept of happiness and related notions. The essence of happiness is difficult to pin down, but regardless of whether it is conceived of as the satisfaction of subjective desires or the cultivation of objectively desirable traits of character, individual liberty remains its indispensable prerequisite. And since fulfilling one's desires and developing one's virtues is nothing but actualizing the potential of one's own free will, one might even argue that happiness is essentially nothing but liberty used to its maximum potential.

The fifth set deals with the topics of aesthetics, culture, and taste. Culture is the aesthetic expression of the primacy of the individual, and as such it is incompatible with tribalistic instincts, collectivist sentiments, and other psychological tendencies hostile to personal liberty. Where the creative power of the individual is subjugated to the whims of the masses, culture invariably withers, and this observation alone should put to rest the notion that the survival of "high art" requires political support, that is, subsidization by monopolistic apparatuses of institutionalized violence.

Finally, the sixth set comprises topics such as knowledge, expectations, order, and chaos. Liberty and knowledge flourish together, since the free market – the economic foundation of civilized society – is a perfect vehicle for disseminating dispersed information, including that of a highly local and tacit nature. However, in order to ensure that the flow of knowledge in society remains uninterrupted, its members have to be able to recognize and reject pseudo-knowledge, especially that which promises to replace the free market system with something supposedly more "rationally planned" or "scientifically organized". Believing such promises, no matter how appealing they may sound, invariably leads to the replacement of the spontaneous order of voluntary exchange with the planned chaos of coercive takings. This is why it is so crucial to cultivate the virtue of common sense, which makes it possible to distinguish between wisdom and sophistry, and thus preserve both the pursuit of genuine knowledge and the enjoyment of genuine liberty.

As indicated in the opening paragraphs of this preface, liberty is an elusive, multifaceted concept, whose understanding requires investigating its content from a variety of perspectives. At the same time, it is the defining feature of human nature, whose appreciation and exploration is the key to material, intellectual, and moral progress of our civilization. Thus, there is no more perennially urgent educational task than spreading the message of liberty as widely as possible. It is my hope that in the context of bringing this task to completion, the terseness of an aphorism can complement the comprehensiveness of a philosophical treatise and the poignancy of a novel. In other words, it is my hope that the message of liberty – the pith of our life – is well suited to be conveyed in a literary form that, at its best, is as pithy as it is lively.

ENTREPRENEURSHIP, BUSINESS, ECONOMICS, AND POLITICS

A bad economist believes that he knows what to do to make the world prosperous. A good economist believes that he knows what to do to let the world make itself prosperous.

A bad economist believes that pay can be legislated. A good economist believes that legislation can be paid for.

A bad economist believes that prices should be policed by the state. A good economist believes that police should be priced by the market.

A businessman calls himself boss, but his goal is to serve others. A politician calls himself servant, but his goal is to boss others.

A fool believes in designing markets. A person of reason believes in marketing designs.

A fool believes that the market makes profits corrupting. A person of reason knows that it makes corruption unprofitable.

A fool deplores the fact that automation destroys jobs. A person of reason delights in the fact that it makes jobs less automatic.

A good economist believes that his role is to improve the public's understanding of the market. A bad economist believes that his role is to improve the market's understanding of the public.

4

A good economist believes that the ones best suited to deal with the problem of scarcity are entrepreneurs. A bad economist believes that it's the economists.

A "guaranteed profit" is something akin to a riskless danger.

A "mathematical economist" is someone too innumerate to be a mathematician, too technically inept to be a natural scientist, too reality-averse to be an insurance broker, and too narcissistic to be an accountant.

A successful speculator is someone who can consistently identify temporary islands of predictability in a vast ocean of randomness.

A technocrat is a philosophically ignorant would-be economist. A utopian is an economically ignorant would-be philosopher.

An economically illiterate ethicist believes that money is the root of all evil. An economically literate ethicist believes that fiat money is the root of much evil.

An economist argues that goods are scarce. A protectionist argues that scarcity is good.

An economist lecturing an entrepreneur on how to make society prosperous is like a grammarian lecturing a novelist on how to write bestsellers.

An entrepreneur is someone who finds a solution before others find a problem. A politician is someone who finds a problem after others find a solution.

An entrepreneur is someone who sees a gain from trade where others see a tradeoff.

An entrepreneur's advice to the customer is that it is reasonable to understand one's options. A politician's advice to the voter is that it is optional to understand one's reasons.

An ethically literate economist believes that ought implies can. An economically illiterate ethicist believes that can implies ought.

Bad economics teaches that computers can design markets. Good economics teaches that markets can design computers.

Bad economics teaches that economies can be planned. Good economics teaches that plans can be economical.

Bad economics teaches that under laissez-faire, employers would discriminate on the basis of race and sex. Good economics teaches than under laissez-faire, employers would have to discriminate on the basis of productivity.

Bad economics teaches that without the state, monopolies would destroy the market. Good economics teaches that without the state, the market would destroy monopolies.

Bastiat and Hazlitt: economics for dummies. Marx and Keynes: economics by dummies.

Believing that a central bank is an element of the free market is like believing that a censorship office is a vehicle of free speech.

Believing that the role of central banks is to fight inflation is like believing that the role of bootleggers is to fight alcoholism.

Blaming speculators for financial crises is like blaming weathermen for natural disasters.

Commerce is an attempt to overcome barbarism. Politics is an attempt to sugarcoat barbarism.

Commerce is reciprocal philanthropy. Politics is reciprocal misanthropy.

Commerce is the bridge between liberty and peace.

Criticizing advertising for creating desires is like criticizing opportunities for creating incentives.

Economics explains the logic of scarcity. Politics explains the scarcity of logic.

Economics is a sound understanding of the logic of human action. Entrepreneurship is a sound application of the logic of human action.

Economics is to ethics what prudence is to justice.

Economics is to politics what education is to brainwashing.

Economics may be a dismal science, but politics is a dismal superstition.

Entrepreneurs make profits by serving the needy. Politicians make profits by creating the needy.

Entrepreneurs take special care in serving singular interests. Politicians take singular care in serving special interests.

Entrepreneurship is practical anarchy. Politics is impractical anarchy.

Entrepreneurship is the art of bringing people together by appealing to their self-interest. Politics is the art of pitting people against each other by appealing to their benevolence.

Entrepreneurship is the art of turning strangers into collaborators. Politics is the art of turning neighbors into enemies.

Entrepreneurship is the creative destruction of scarcity. Politics is the destructive creation of scarcity.

Entrepreneurship is the use of self-interest in the service of others. Politics is the use of others in the service of self-interest.

Every call to constrain the "unbridled" market is an endorsement of the crudity of concentrated ignorance over the subtlety of dispersed knowledge.

Expressing fear that cheap foreign labor will "steal" one's job is the most disarmingly honest admission of professional incompetence.

Fiat money is to finance what a nuke is to warfare.

Fiat money: the gold standard of counterfeit.

Free trade is the process whereby people become friends without even being acquaintances.

"Free-market monopoly" is something akin to "competitive government bureaucracy".

Good economics teaches that scarcity can be reduced. Bad economics teaches that scarcity can be eliminated. In other words, good economics tries to harness the logic of human action, while bad economics tries to ignore it.

Government investment in entrepreneurship is something akin to a Luddite's investment in automation.

If you have a problem, an entrepreneur will do his best to offer you a solution. If you have a solution, a politician will do his best to offer you a problem.

Inflation: the invisible hand of legal plunder.

Interventionism: the art of putting out fires with the use of gasoline.

Interventionism: the art of turning the blessings of private ownership into the tragedy of the commons.

Interventionism: the idea that the best way to improve the efficiency of peaceful producers is to submit them to the control of aggressive parasites.

It takes the stupidity of a simpleton to believe that socialism can work, but it takes the stupidity of an intellectual to believe that he can make socialism work.

It takes the stupidity of a simpleton to grumble about the inefficiency of capitalism, but it takes the stupidity of an intellectual to praise the efficiency of socialism.

Keynesianism: the curious notion that spending the unearned can result in earning the unspendable.

Keynesianism: the long-run death of the economy.

Keynesianism: the notion that the actions of frugal producers should be managed by a giant spendthrift parasite.

Laissez-faire is not based on the exaggerated claim that every market entrepreneur is a hero and every state bureaucrat is a villain, but on the prudent observation that the free market is the most fertile breeding ground for heroes, while state politics is the most fertile breeding ground for villains.

Ludwig von Mises
smashed socialism to pieces.
Reason saved the day.

Market anarchism: the common sense idea that the most effective way to reduce the scale of violence is to get rid of the only entity that can legally pay for its outbursts of violence out of everyone else's pockets.

Market anarchy is order without orders. Political tyranny is rule without rules.

Market failure contains the seeds of its own correction. Government failure contains the seeds of its own perpetuation.

Markets make it rational to be rational. Politics makes it foolish not to be foolish.

Marxism is the opium of economic illiterates.

Perhaps the reason why market failures are discussed more often than government failures is that there are also market successes.

Pleading for government to revive a depressed economy is like pleading for an arsonist to lead a fire brigade.

Political correctness suggests that laissez-faire threatens the economy. Economic correctness suggests that laissez-faire threatens politics.

Politics is a perpetual tragedy of the commons writ large. Entrepreneurship is a perpetual coordination game writ large.

Politics is about helping oneself in the name of helping others. Business is about helping others in the name of helping oneself.

Politics is about making promises that cannot be delivered. Entrepreneurship is about delivering on the promises that do not have to be made.

Politics is an attempt to achieve individual gains by exploiting collective madness. Entrepreneurship is an attempt to achieve collective gains by exploiting individual rationality.

Politics is an attempt to legitimize the evil side of human nature. Entrepreneurship is an attempt to turn it to good use.

Politics is the art of disguising vices as virtues. Entrepreneurship is the art of turning vices into virtues.

Politics is the art of organizing collective hatreds. Entrepreneurship is the art of breaking them down in the name of mutual benefit.

Politics is the intrusion of zero-sum thinking into a positive-sum world. Entrepreneurship is the infusion of positive-sum thinking into a zero-sum world.

Politics is the process of infecting human affairs with organized violence. Entrepreneurship is the process of imbuing human affairs with organized harmony.

Private property is the bridge between liberty and prosperity.

Private provision of goods depends on entrepreneurs' willingness to generate profits. "Public" provision of goods depends on entrepreneurs' tolerance for being robbed of profits.

Protectionism: the notion that the way to achieve global success is to subsidize provincial failure.

"Public property": the private "property" of expropriators.

Saying that certain branches of the economy are too important to be privatized is like saying that certain parts of the body are too important to be resuscitated.

Saying that market entrepreneurs owe their profits to the state because they use "public services" is like saying that chattel slaves owe allegiance to their master because they are fed and sheltered by him.

Saying that property is theft makes as much sense as saying that marriage is adultery.

Social progress is the process of substituting commerce for conquest.

Speculator: someone whose insight is mistaken for cheating by those who mistake their ignorance for honesty.

Subsidizing entrepreneurship is something akin to standardizing creativity.

The belief that consumption drives the economy is like the belief that the best way to multiply one's wealth is to fritter it away.

The belief that government can be run like a business is like the belief that a brothel can be run like a convent.

The belief that government spending can stimulate the economy is like the belief that bloodletting can alleviate anemia.

The belief that the minimum wage law can reduce poverty is like the belief that flogging a dead horse can turn it into a living unicorn.

The best measure of something's uselessness is the amount of subsidies that sustain its existence.

The choice is never between economic planning and economic chaos, but always between bottom-up planning by enterprising makers and top-down planning by bureaucratic bunglers.

The choice is never between order and anarchy, but between the orderly anarchy of the market and the chaotic anarchy of politics.

The difference between a customer and a voter is that the former chooses between scarce goods, while the latter chooses between free bads.

The difference between an entrepreneur and a charlatan is that the former predicts his sales, while the latter sells his predictions.

The difference between the ruthlessness of the market and the ruthlessness of politics is that the market ruthlessly punishes stupidity, while politics ruthlessly promotes it.

The first step on the road to abundance is the understanding of scarcity.

The globalization of free trade is world peace in the making.

The goal of a politician is to make his constituents an offer they can't refuse. The goal of an entrepreneur is to make his customers an offer they can't resist.

The greatest threat to political power is not a revolutionary mob or an invading army, but an expanding black market.

The intellectual foundation of social progress is the process of debunking positive myths about power and negative myths about liberty.

The invisible hand of the market makes prosperity ubiquitous. The ubiquitous hand of the state makes prosperity invisible.

The market is a vehicle for channeling individual ambitions into collective benefits. The state is a vehicle for channeling individual resentments into collective tragedies.

The market is an expression of society's collective knowledge. Politics is an expression of its collective ignorance.

The market is organized peace in the service of mutual gain. The state is organized violence in the service of mutual plunder.

The market is the institutional expression of peoples' cooperative reasons. The state is the institutional expression of their plundering instincts.

The market is the most highly organized form of modern civilization. The state is the most highly organized form of primeval barbarism.

The market makes mistakes, but the state is a mistake.

The market may be unable to eliminate scarcity, but the state is unrivaled in creating it.

The market may be unable to make everyone happy, but the state is more than able to make everyone miserable.

The message of economics is that it is impossible to get something for nothing. The message of politics is that it is all too possible to get nothing for something.

The message of economics is that options are real. The message of politics is that reality is optional.

The message of economics is to think on the margin. The message of politics is to marginalize thinking.

The message of politics is that scarcity can be legislated out of existence. The message of economics is that scarcity can be legislated into existence.

The message of politics is that some forms of subjection are better than others. The message of economics is that any form of cooperation is better that every form of subjection.

The most basic public good is freedom from public do-gooders.

The role of economics is to explain the difference between the possible and the desirable. The role of politics is to deny it.

The role of politics is to advertise utopias. The role of economics is to shoot them down.

The role of politics is to create conflict by talking about the common good. The role of entrepreneurship is to resolve conflict by making goods common.

The state is the ultimate collective bully. The market is the ultimate collective peacemaker.

The state supervising the market is something akin to a pickpocket supervising a shopkeeper.

The task of an entrepreneur is to make clever choices between opportunities. The task of a politician is to make clever choices between opportunisms.

The task of economics is to point our attention to the unseen. The task of politics is to divert our attention away from it.

The task of economics is to reveal the hidden order of society. The task of politics is to hide the naked chaos of the state.

The task of politics is to demonstrate what is the best way to plunder each other. The task of economics is to demonstrate that to plunder each other is not the best way.

The ultimate proof that businesspeople care about more than money and power is that if they didn't, they would be politicians.

The victory of the market over the state is the victory of mutual profit over mutual plunder.

The world will know peace when the only borders left are those of legitimate property.

To believe that government can correct market failure is to believe that a caveman's club can fix a broken quantum computer.

To substitute economics for politics is to substitute peace for conflict.

Uncertainty and scarcity are the parents of opportunity.

War can end economic depression only in the same way as death can end illness.

When was the last time you heard someone say "the market should do something about it"?

World peace is free trade taken to its logical conclusion.

Worrying about the trade deficit is like worrying that you cannot remember the last time you supplied your local grocery store.

LIBERTY, AUTHORITY, AND POWER

A barbarian believes in coercion as a means to establish cooperation. A civilized person believes in cooperation as a means to eliminate coercion.

A barbarian believes in the benevolence of power. A civilized person believes in the power of benevolence.

A barbarian believes that liberty erodes community. A civilized person knows that liberty creates community.

A collectivist in a libertarian society may be an odd duck, but an individualist in a statist society can only be a milk cow.

A consistent freedom lover is an anarchist in the making.

A democratic state is a device for feeding off society by pitting it against itself.

A democratic state is a device whereby everyone gets a chance to assert his nuisance value on a social scale.

A democratic statist is someone who believes that individual liberty consists in participation in the process of collective self-enslavement.

A fool believes that individual liberty can be established by means of political power. A person of reason believes that political power can be abolished by means of individual liberty.

A fool believes that liberty comes from participation in power. A person of reason knows that it comes from dissipation of power.

A fool believes that the fundamental class struggle is between proletarians and plutocrats. A person of reason knows that it is between libertarians and bureaucrats.

A fool believes that the state is what prevents society from falling into the hands of bandits. A person of reason knows that the state is what results from society falling into the hands of bandits.

A fool believes that the state of nature is a war of all against all. A person of reason knows that the war of all against all is the nature of the state.

A fool believes that without the state, people would be at the mercy of petty criminals. A person of reason knows that without the state, people wouldn't be at the mercy of gigantic criminals.

A free life can be evil, but an unfree life can't be good.

A free man believes that he has rights. A slave believes that he deserves rights.

A free man believes that he is free. A slave believes that he is allowed to be free.

A free society is one in which rules are made by owners, not by controllers.

A genuine slave hates the freedom of others more than his own subjugation. A genuine free person enjoys the freedom of others just as much as his own.

A libertarian is someone who graduated from thinking that there are problems with the state to realizing that the state is the problem.

A libertarian is someone who lacks the talent to rationalize legal plunder.

A libertarian is someone who rejects the curious notion that the common good requires common violence.

A limited government is, logically speaking, something akin to a limited pandemic.

A minarchist is someone who is happy to lock himself in a cell with a psychopathic killer as soon as the latter solemnly promises to beat him only once a month and do it exceedingly gently.

A minimal state is a maximal state in the making.

A perfect slave does not believe that slavery is good, but that it is inevitable. He does not believe that liberty is bad, but that it is impossible.

A perfect slave is someone who believes that liberty is the ability to manage one's own cage.

A politician pledging allegiance to liberty is something akin to a prostitute taking a vow of chastity.

A prisoner is someone who lost his liberty. A slave is someone who gave it away.

A real slave is not someone whose freedom is constrained, but someone who feels constrained by his freedom.

A secularist is someone who advocates the separation of church and state. A libertarian is someone who advocates the separation of society and state.

A slave believes that liberty consists in being able to get permission to rule oneself. A free person believes that it consists in not being able to get permission to rule others.

A slave believes that liberty consists in choosing one's masters. A free person believes that it consists in mastering one's choices.

A slave believes that liberty is the price of security. A free person knows that it is its foundation.

A slave believes that security is a prerequisite of liberty. A free person knows that liberty is a prerequisite of security.

A slave believes that the law should define the scope of liberty. A free person believes that liberty should define the scope of the law.

A slave demands happiness. A free man pursues it.

A slave identifies the state with society. A free person replaces the state with society.

A slave is someone who believes that freedom is the state of being ruled in the right way. A free person is someone who knows that the state of being ruled in any way is slavery.

A slave unquestioningly yields to authority. A free person unyieldingly questions authority.

A society without rules is like a body deprived of nutrients. A society without rulers is like a body free of parasites.

A statist accusing a libertarian of believing in simplistic solutions is like a pickpocket accusing an investor of believing in get-rich-quick schemes.

A statist is someone who believes that nothing promotes the sense of community like the threat of organized violence.

A statist is someone who believes that the perfect vehicle for committing evil will attract the perfect candidates for promoting good.

A statist is someone who feels threatened by a monopolistic audiobook seller, but feels protected by a monopolistic drone striker.

A supporter of the state believes in liberation through power. A supporter of society believes in empowerment through liberty.

A thief just steals. A hypocrite just lies. A hoodlum just bullies. Not many can boast the versatility of politicians.

A typical statist is someone who believes that the fantastically hypothetical threat of a corporation monopolizing the supply of water is a devastating objection to libertarianism, but the painfully real threat of a state methodically exterminating tens of millions of individuals is not a devastating objection to statism.

A utopian anarchist aims to destroy political power. A pragmatic anarchist aims to make it irrelevant.

A utopian anarchist believes that since humans are inherently good, no government is necessary. A pragmatic anarchist believes that since humans are not inherently good, no government is desirable.

A violent market is a possibility, but a violent state is a pleonasm.

A voluntary society is not one in which people became saints, but one in which they stopped obeying villains.

A voluntary society is not one in which there are no criminals, but one in which no criminals are worshipped.

Abolitionism was a movement to end private slavery. Libertarianism is a movement to end private and public slavery.

Anarchism: the scary notion that no one should be exempted from the principle of non-aggression.

Anarchist: a conspiracy theorist who believes that the point of subjecting people to monopolized violence is to exploit rather than serve them.

Anarchist: someone curiously resistant to the brilliant notion that the way to stay protected from violence is to submit to its rule.

An anarchist is a minarchist who takes secession seriously.

An anarchist is someone who followed the trail of freedom to its logical conclusion.

An anarchist is someone who lost the ability to make excuses for legalized thuggery.

An anarchist is someone who rejects the curious notion that crimes become virtues as they grow in size.

An attempt to rationalize aggression is an encouragement to aggress against rationality.

Barbarism replaced by civilization is called society. Barbarism disguised as civilization is called the state.

Begging the state for protection from the "ruthlessness of the market" is like begging a murderer for protection from the hustle and bustle of life.

Believing that politics can advance the cause of liberty is like believing that quackery can advance the cause of health.

Believing that the function of politics is to resolve conflicts is like believing that the function of gasoline is to put out fires.

Believing that the state is the safeguard of society is like believing that plunder is the safeguard of prosperity.

Calling a libertarian a hypocrite for traveling on highways is like calling an abolitionist a hypocrite for wearing cotton socks.

Calling upon the state to stop the spread of violence is like calling upon a virus to stop the spread of a disease.

Civilization is the process of substituting liberty for power.

Civilization will truly begin the day the belief in the right to rule is truly gone.

Claiming that a stateless society is bound to turn into a battleground for warlords makes as much sense as claiming that a slaveless society is bound to turn into a hunting ground for slave-catchers.

Consistent interventionism is totalitarianism in the making.

Constitution: the minimal state's fig leaf for maximal statism.

Crony politics is not an aberration, but a tautology.

Demanding an exact blueprint for a free society is like demanding a deterministic algorithm for spontaneous creativity.

Democracy is a device for sugarcoating slavery by convincing the slaves that they are each other's masters.

Democracy is a tool for preserving collective violence by inviting everyone to participate in it. Liberty is a tool for dissolving collective violence by making the invitees pay for the mess that they make.

Democracy is everyone having a share in power. Liberty is no one having a share in power.

Democracy is liberty to choose one's preferred form of enslavement. Liberty is the ability to make this choice irrelevant.

Democracy is the freedom to choose authorities. Autonomy is the authority to choose freedom.

Democracy is to liberty as pyrite is to gold.

Democracy: the notion that the sheep can control the wolves when given the option of joining the wolf pack.

Election: an all-pay auction of bads.

Election: the tragicomedy of the commons.

Expecting monopolized violence to protect liberty is like expecting pandemics to have therapeutic effects.

First and foremost, liberty is the ability to refuse the status quo.

Governments represent their citizens in the same way as parasites represent their hosts.

"Heroism" is the most common euphemism for the bloodlust of the state's enforcers.

If it looks like a politician, sounds like a politician, and acts like a politician, then it probably is a psychopathic crook.

If men were angels, no government would be necessary, but since they are not, no government is desirable.

If one believes that organization requires coercion, then coercion is the only thing one will be able to organize.

If the social contract can be made in the state of nature, then the state is redundant. If the social contract cannot be made in the state of nature, then the state is impossible. If no social contract is in fact made in the state of nature, then the state is unjustified. If no social contract needs to be made in the state of nature, then the state is a fiction.

If to be human is to think and choose for oneself, then to be governed is to be labeled subhuman.

If you claim that violence is necessary to keep society together, you prove that you have no idea what society is.

If you think that nothing can accomplish the feat of simultaneously insulting one's intellect, conscience, and taste, think back no further than any election campaign.

If you want peace, do not ask how institutional violence can be used to eliminate defiance, but how defiance can be used to eliminate institutional violence.

Individualism is the seed of liberty. Cooperation is its fruit.

Interventionism: the art of blaming liberty for the failures of coercion.

It takes instinct to obey authority. It takes reason to question it.

It takes intelligence to appreciate one's liberty, but it takes wisdom to appreciate the liberty of others.

Justice without law is called integrity. Law without justice is called politics.

Libertarian: someone inexplicably skeptical of the notion that the greatest experts in bullying the weak are the greatest experts in helping the needy.

Libertarianism: color-blind abolitionism.

Libertarianism is a constant reminder that the king is not only naked, but also reeking of death.

Libertarianism is not a call to revolutionize politics, but an invitation to transcend it.

Libertarianism is to statism what abolitionism is to slavery.

Libertarianism: the idea that the best form of government is that of the individual over himself.

Libertarianism: the idea that voluntarily wasting one's life does not justify coercively wasting the lives of others.

Libertarianism: the only social philosophy that does not discriminate in favor of aggression.

Libertarianism: the radical notion that collective action need not mean collective violence.

Liberty begins with the recognition that there is no such thing as the right to rule.

Liberty does not guarantee solutions, but coercion guarantees problems.

Liberty is not a recipe for a good life, but the only opportunity to avoid a miserable one.

Liberty is not sufficient to find the meaning of life, but it is necessary to live a life of meaning.

Liberty is the mother of all virtues, but the midwife of none.

Liberty offers nothing but the chance to try everything.

Minarchism is the curious idea that bunglers and bullies are not to be trusted, except in matters of greatest importance.

Minarchism: the idea that it is smart to walk into the open jaws of a carnivorous monster as soon as it solemnly declares itself a vegetarian.

Minarchism: the idea that it is utopian to think that a carnivorous monster can be starved to death, but it is pragmatic to think that it can be turned into a vegetarian.

One of the most common and most treacherous mistakes that a libertarian can make is to be more against statism than in favor of liberty.

"Political authority" is the only thing that cannot be mocked enough.

Politics is an endless, borderless war against individual liberty.

Politics is the art of cultivating Stockholm syndromes.

Politics is the art of ruining the world while coming across as its savior.

"Positive liberty" is the mother of all Orwellianisms.

Power excites, but liberty inspires.

Power is the liberty to oppress the weak. Liberty is the power to weaken the oppressors.

"Public interest": the interest of those who use collective fictions to subdue individual realities.

"Public interest": the private interest of someone who believes that someone else's private interest can be sacrificed to pursue it.

Redistribution: the curious notion that the best way to better the situation of those who need help is to allow oneself to be robbed by those who crave power.

Redistribution: the transfer of property from each according to his political innocence to each according to his lobbying influence.

Representative democracy: the curious notion that to be free is to periodically rubber-stamp your enslavement.

Requiring no justification for individual liberty is the defining characteristic of an inherently civilized person.

Rules are a manifestation of spontaneous order. Rulers are a manifestation of planned chaos.

Saying "gun control is needed to prevent gun violence" is like saying "a civil war is needed to prevent barroom brawls".

Saying "people are not angels, so we need a government to watch them" is like saying "sociopaths with guns are dangerous, so let us allow them to have tanks and nuclear weapons".

Saying that it is pointless to try to build a voluntary society since there will always be criminals is like saying that it is pointless to respect your neighbor's property since there will always be robbers.

Saying that one is willing to give up liberty for security is like saying that one is willing to give up life for a life jacket.

Secession: the process whereby leviathans are reduced to leprechauns.

Seek liberty in power, and you will find neither. Seek power in liberty, and you will find both.

Slave: someone who prefers free goods to free choice.

Slavery begins with the belief that in order to secure freedom, some must be free to restrict the freedom of others. Freedom begins with the belief that in order to eliminate slavery, all must be free to oppose the restrictions of others.

Slavery: full employment minus full consent.

Slaves desire leaders. Free people desire partners.

"Social contract": the notion that the best way to protect one's freedom is to voluntarily turn into a slave.

Social order is a coordinated network of individual anarchies.

Social progress is the process of substituting rules for rulers.

Society is a device for eliminating violence by ostracizing anyone who participates in it. The state is a device for whitewashing violence by inviting everyone to participate in it.

Society is a reflection of peoples' individual virtues. The state is a reflection of their collective vices.

Society is a voluntary scheme of mutual benefit. The state is a compulsory scheme of mutual exploitation.

Society is based on the belief that cooperation trumps violence. The state is based on the belief that cooperation requires violence.

Society is cooperation against plunder. The state is cooperation in plunder.

Society is the greatest opportunity cost of the state.

Statehood is the ultimate dream of every ambitious protection racket.

Statism is a virus that infects the spontaneous order of society with the planned chaos of politics.

Statism is the belief that the way to deal with evil is not to fight it, but to institutionalize it. In other words, it is the belief that the way to make evil disappear is not to counter it with good, but to paint it as good.

Statism: anarchism for the privileged.

Statism is the continuation of slavery by other means.

Statism is the idea that the best fire insurance policy is to give arsonists the exclusive right to use matches.

Statism is the most highly organized form of tribal savagery.

Statism: the belief that a comparative advantage in violence is more likely to imply a comparative advantage in protection than a comparative advantage in plunder.

Statism: the belief that the only alternative to the utopia of peace is the dystopia of violence.

Statism: the belief that you require permission to be free.

Statism: the idea that aggression should be in charge of peace.

Statism: the practice of sacrificing individual reasons on the altar of collective superstitions.

The advocacy of a voluntary society is not founded on the utopian hope that people will start loving good, but on the modest expectation that they may stop praising evil.

The best way to swallow the humiliation of being ruled by idiots is to imagine being ruled by intellectuals.

The blessing of the human species is that it can appreciate liberty. The tragedy of the human species is that it can fear it.

The choice between liberty and obedience is the choice between the risk of failure and the certainty of it.

The choice is never between absolute freedom and regulation, but between regulation by the customer and regulation by the plunderer.

The choice is never between liberty and security, but always between the security of liberty and the danger of enslavement.

The choice is never between order and anarchy, but between the order of power and the order of liberty, that is, between anarchy for rulers and anarchy for all.

The claim that liberty is not the only value is nearly always a thinly veiled threat of delegated violence.

The claim that liberty must be restricted rarely includes the liberty of the claimant.

The "consent of the governed" is something akin to the autonomy of the enslaved.

The difference between a barbarian and a civilized person is that the former is willing to do what is legal even if it is immoral, while the latter is willing to do what is moral even if it is illegal.

The difference between an anarchist and a ruler is that the ruler believes in anarchy exclusively for the rulers.

The difference between reluctantly suffering power and willingly collaborating with it is the difference between keeping what remains of one's liberty and losing what remains of one's dignity.

The difference between the state and the mafia is that the mafia doesn't demand the gratitude of its victims.

The essential feature of moral stupidity is the belief that good results can be coerced into existence.

The establishment of a voluntary society will not be the culmination of human history, but the true beginning of its non-barbaric part.

The excuse of a petty tyrant is that he needs to protect himself against you. The excuse of a great tyrant is that he needs to protect you against yourself.

The first step in giving peace the power to eliminate violence is to reject the belief in the power of violence to preserve peace.

The first step in ridding society of violence is to stop believing that it is threats of violence that keep it together.

The first step in substituting cooperation for coercion is to stop believing that cooperation requires coercion.

The first step towards eliminating violence is to stop confusing it with protection.

The goal of libertarianism is not to offer social solutions, but to allow every member of society to seek them.

The goal of libertarianism is not to permit people to be free, but to make them realize that they don't need anyone's permission to be free.

The goal of libertarianism is not to solve the problems of politics, but to show that the problem is politics.

The goal of libertarianism is to replace violence with cooperation. The goal of statism is to disguise violence as cooperation.

The goal of society is to advance the power of progress. The goal of the state is to advance the progress of power.

The greatest moral achievement of most people is that they never became politicians.

The greatest obstacle to eliminating violence is not its actual evil, but the belief in its potential for good.

The greatest obstacle to liberty is not that some want to be masters, but that so many don't mind being slaves.

The greatest tragedy of statism is not that billions are subjected to the rule of violence, but that they can hardly imagine a more natural state of affairs.

The guiding principle of a slave is to fear liberty. The guiding principle of a free person is to liberate oneself from fear.

The inherent social conflict is not between the rich and the poor, the employers and the employees, the natives and the immigrants, the puritans and the hedonists, or the majority and the minority, but between the state and society, that is, between organized violence and organized liberty.

The intellectual foundation of libertarianism is a simple recognition of the fact that the methods of primeval barbarism cannot solve the problems of modern civilization.

The message of ethics is that the greater the evil, the greater the tragedy. The message of politics is that the greater the evil, the greater the opportunity.

The message of libertarianism is a constant reminder that aggression by any other name smells just as rotten.

The metaphysical foundational of every form of statism is the belief in an omnipotent secular god of violence.

The more stately the state, the less social the society.

The most common symptom of barbarism is the inability to distinguish between disapproval and prohibition.

The most common symptom of mental slavery is the belief in a tradeoff between liberty and community.

The most dangerous kind of violence is the one that can successfully pass itself off as protection.

The most defining feature of a barbaric mind is the belief that violence is the best guarantee of success.

The most effective way for the state to enslave society is to impersonate it.

The most effective way to destroy society is to legislate its functions.

The most effective way to make slavery appealing is to make the slavemaster an elective office.

The most effective way to make society stupid is to allow it to be tinkered with by intellectuals.

The most essential social choice is not between individualism and collectivism, capitalism and socialism, autocracy and democracy, consumerism and asceticism, or conservatism and progressivism, but between voluntariness and coercion.

The most important step on the road to liberty is not to defy one's master, but to stop believing that it is normal to have one.

The most obvious reason why the world is not a better place is that nearly all of its otherwise intelligent and principled inhabitants believe that the thing that holds it together is monopolized violence, aggression, and plunder.

The most potent source of mental slavery is the unthinking belief in the greatness of one's nation.

The most socially damaging myth is the belief that collective action requires centralized coercion.

The only common good is the common liberty to pursue individual goods.

The only compromise between individualism and statism is to have as many states as there are individuals.

The only consolation of being ruled by cynics is not being ruled by idealists.

The only public good is freedom from being subjected to anyone's private vision of what public good is.

The only way to prevent anything from being ruled is to make everything owned.

The opposite of tyranny is not democracy, but liberty. The opposite of privilege is not equality, but autonomy. The opposite of oppression is not welfare, but charity. And the opposite of barbarism is not the state, but society.

The persistent belief in "good government" is the most destructive form of moral masochism.

The progress of individual liberty is the process whereby the instinct of violence is replaced by the logic of peace.

The psychological foundation of every form of statism is the perverse satisfaction of belonging to the gang of the biggest neighborhood bully.

The "regulatory" state is the totalitarian state in slow motion.

The role of ethics is to separate evil from good. The role of politics is to disguise evil as good.

The role of liberty is not to make life good, but to allow it to be good.

The role of liberty is not to solve problems, but to make them solvable.

The state is a device for turning protection into intimidation, cooperation into exploitation, education into indoctrination, entrepreneurship into rent-seeking, and loyalty into submission.

The state is a device for whitewashing evil by making its acceptance popular, its perpetration vicarious, its causes impersonal, and its effects remote.

The state is the ultimate manifestation of the barbaric belief in the omnipotent power of organized violence.

The tragedy of homo sapiens is that he is free by nature, but a slave by instinct.

The ultimate example of adding insult to injury is to suggest to the plundered that there is an implicit social contract between themselves and the plunderers.

The vision of a free society is not based on the utopian hope that violence will disappear, but on the modest expectation that it will stop being glorified.

The world will know peace when hostilities between states are replaced by hostility against statism.

There is no tradeoff between liberty and security, unless what is meant is the liberty of the ruled and the security of the rulers.

To accept being ruled may be a matter of prudence, but to enjoy being ruled is only a matter of shame.

To be a hero is not to sacrifice one's liberty for the collective, but to defend it against the collective.

To be a libertarian is to be consistent in one's condemnation of aggressive violence.

To believe that there is such a thing as the right to rule is to disbelieve that civilized living is possible.

To call for good government is to call for a benevolent slave master. To call for good governance is to call for a prudent collaborator.

To call politics "applied ethics" is not to dignify politics, but to insult ethics.

To confuse society with the state is to confuse the control of violence with the violence of control.

To mistake aggression for protection is to protect aggression.

To mistake the power of the state for the power of society is to mistake the voracity of a parasite for the vitality of its host.

To win a conflict, side with power. To resolve a conflict, side with liberty.

Today's believer in the impossibility of libertarianism is yesterday's believer in the inevitability of slavery.

Total war is statism taken to its logical conclusion.

Using the word "we" on behalf of strangers is the first step towards mental totalitarianism.

Violence can make one a captive, but it is only submission to violence that can make one a slave.

Voter: someone free to choose the form of his subjection.

War is a conflict of states. Peace is a harmony of anarchies.

War is born in the belief that organized violence is necessary to preserve liberty. Peace is born in the belief that organized liberty is necessary to defeat violence.

Welfare statism: the idea that being responsible for others requires destroying the freedom of others to be responsible for themselves.

What a statist calls "anarchy" is a dysfunctional state. What an anarchist calls "anarchy" is a functional absence of the state.

What distinguishes a civilized person from a barbarian is not verbal skills, technological development, or appreciation of the arts, but genuine respect for personal liberty.

Whenever someone says that if men were angels, no government would be necessary, ask him which angel he most likes to be governed by.

World peace will come about when every shout "it's an order!" will be countered with a shrug.

MONEY, GREED, EQUALITY, ENVY, AND CHARITY

A civilized person believes that what matters is not whether wealth is equally distributed, but whether it is justly acquired. A barbarian believes that the latter depends on the former.

A fool believes that people are free when they are all equal. A person of reason believes that people are equal when they are all free.

A fool believes that taxes are the price we pay for a civilized society. A person of reason knows that a civilized society is the price we pay for taxes.

A fool complains about the lack of equality of opportunity. A person of reason appreciates the abundance of diversity of opportunity.

A fool deplores the fact that without the state, the poor would be at the mercy of individual charity. A person of reason delights in the fact that without the state, the poor wouldn't be at the mercy of institutional violence.

A fool finds intolerable the inequality of wealth between the capitalist and the laborer. A person of reason finds intolerable the inequality of rights between the state and the individual.

A foolish egalitarian wants to empower the state to prevent the market from making the rich richer. A smart egalitarian wants to empower the market to prevent the state from keeping the poor poor.

A foolish environmentalist wants to save nature from the greed of the market by exposing it to the tragedy of the commons. A smart environmentalist wants to save nature from the tragedy of the commons by exposing it to the greed of the market.

A "just tax" is something akin to an "affectionate rape".

A libertarian does not oppose the welfare state because he does not care about the poor, but because he cares about them too much to believe they deserve being caught in the web of lies, empty promises, perpetual dependence, hate-mongering, and cultural degradation created by self-serving, power-hungry crooks.

A petty robber profits by stealing money. A great robber profits by creating money.

A petty robber steals amid the silence of the night. A great robber steals amid the applause of the crowd.

A petty robber's excuse is that he needs your money to help himself. A great robber's excuse is that he needs your money to help you.

A pickpocket is to a central banker what an amateur is to a virtuoso.

A slave believes that the choice is between individualistic selfishness and collectivist solidarity. A free person knows that it is between individual charity and collective parasitism.

A welfare state is a bankrupt state in the making.

Active charity: giving money to philanthropic organizations.
Passive charity: keeping money out of the hands of the state.

An entrepreneur is greedy for the money that you are willing to give him. A politician is greedy for the money that you want to keep for yourself.

Benevolence is based on the belief that charity is right. Parasitism is based on the belief that charity is a right.

Bureaucrat: a selfless do-gooder, conscientious and self-abnegating to the point of making his concerned beneficiaries secretly pay him to enjoy an occasional moment of rest.

Business is the use of individual greed in the service of collective wealth. Politics is the use of individual wealth in the service of collective greed.

Coerced virtue is something akin to rape-induced love.

Critics of consumerism are very serious people as long as they remain in their monastic cells.

Democracy: a system that brings people together by thrusting their hands into each other's pockets.

Denouncing the supposed greed of the rich is the surest sign of greed for riches.

Egalitarianism is the sex appeal of envy.

Egalitarianism: the meritocracy of losers.

Egoist: someone who won't let me parasitize on him.

Envy: a poor man's greed.

Fairness is the belief in the equality of justice. Envy is the belief in the justice of equality.

"Free": costly in an unobvious way.

Gratitude: the realization that charity is not a right.

Greed is the envy of the winner. Envy is the greed of the loser.

Greed is when your neighbor satisfies his need. Need is when you satisfy your greed.

Greed: the ambition of the envied.

If people are caring, then the welfare state is a hindrance. If they are uncaring, then the welfare state is a hoax.

If politicians were smart and benevolent, they would be philanthropists or high-level charity workers. If they were dull and benevolent, they would be low-level charity workers. If they were smart and malevolent, they would be oligarchic puppet masters. If they were dull and malevolent, I don't have to tell you who they would be.

If you say that money does not bring happiness, don't embarrass yourself by saying that unhappiness justifies taking the money of others.

In a free market, the best way to help the poor is to become rich. In a politicized market, the best way to help the rich is to become poor.

Inequality of income is an obvious consequence of the inequality of outcome.

It takes abstract thinking to see how greed can lead to prosperity, but it takes wishful thinking to claim that violence can lead to charity.

It takes casual indifference not to be charitable with one's possessions, but it takes deliberate malice to claim to be charitable with one's plunder.

It takes the stupidity of a simpleton to believe in unconditional income, but it takes the stupidity of an intellectual to promote it as a human right.

Libertarianism cannot promise to save the poor, but statism can promise to corrupt them.

Lovers of humanity are rarely lovers of humans.

Marxism in one sentence: from each according to his wealth, to each according to his envy.

Marxism: the notion that political envy is a substitute for economic knowledge.

Meritocratic inequality of wealth is a sign of civilizational progress, if only for the reason that the pre-civilizational starting point is always equality of poverty.

Plunder a society, and you have made it temporarily poor. Convince its members that they are entitled to plunder each other, and you have made it permanently poor.

Protectionism: the notion that global cooperation should be sacrificed for tribal opportunism.

"Public debt": what the parasites declare productive society owes them.

Redistribution is a self-reinforcing feedback loop of robbing the rich of their wealth to rob the poor of their dignity.

Saying "people before profits" makes as much sense as saying "life before breathing".

Saying that justice demands material equality is a euphemistic way of saying that envy demands material satisfaction.

Saying "the super-rich can buy politicians, therefore we should get rid of the super-rich" is like saying "people can catch syphilis, therefore we should get rid of people".

Society is a device for replacing plunder with charity. The state is a device for disguising plunder as charity.

Statism: the brilliant notion that the way to reduce the power of money is to give more money to power.

Tax avoidance: the process whereby the greed of a businessman saves scarce resources from the greed of a bureaucrat.

Taxation is to theft as war is to murder.

The achievement of the welfare state is the welfare of the state. The cost of the welfare state is the welfare of everyone else.

The belief that there is a tradeoff between liberty and charity can only originate in a mind that is as slavish as it is uncharitable.

The choice is never between basic goods as rights and basic goods as commodities, but between basic goods as objects of exchange and basic goods as objects of plunder.

The claim that money doesn't buy happiness is rarely made by the rich and happy.

The difference between a civilized person and a barbarian is that the former appreciates inequality as a reminder of human diversity, while the latter hates it as a reminder of his inferiority.

The difference between a healthy society and a toxic one is that the members of the former feel grateful for help, while those of the latter feel entitled to it.

The difference between a mugger and an egalitarian is that the former is vile enough to deprive his victims of their property, but he is not mad enough to honestly believe that he thereby repossesses what is rightfully his.

The difference between a philanthropist and a politician is that the former helps others with his money, while the latter helps himself with others' money.

The difference between a philanthropist and a politician is that the former uses his wealth to benefit the needy, while the latter uses the needy to benefit his wealth.

The difference between needs and wants is that the former are mine and the latter yours.

The difference between the state and the welfare state is that the former is content with robbing its victims of their liberty, while the latter does not yield till it robs them of their dignity as well.

The easiest way to refute the notion that business is just greed and corruption is to point out that we can distinguish it from politics.

The first step towards getting help from a stranger is acknowledging that you are not entitled to it.

The market is a device for converting individual greed into collective prosperity. The state is a device for converting collective envy into individual misery.

The more "free" goods, the fewer free people.

The most effective way to destroy solidarity among people is to convince them that it consists in being entitled to live at each other's expense.

The most potent source of spontaneous hatred is compulsory benevolence.

The ones who condemn the "cult of money" are always the ones most eager to grab the money of others.

The state is a device for disguising individual greeds as collective needs. The market is a device for coordinating individual greeds with collective needs.

The surest way to perpetuate poverty is to make it affordable.

The way to make virtue flourish is to practice it. The way to make virtue wither is to legislate it.

The ultimate form of leaving someone without help is teaching him to always expect it.

The welfare state is a device for replacing charity with plunder, compassion with contempt, gratitude with entitlement, dignity with helplessness, admiration with envy, and solidarity with resentment.

The world will know peace when the last government building is turned into a shopping mall.

To legislate against the power of greed is to legislate in favor of the greed of power.

To seek charity is to be temporarily helpless. To feel entitled to charity is to be permanently helpless.

Voter: someone smart enough to manage his country, but not smart enough to manage his wallet.

Welfare statism: the notion that the best way to gain the political support of those deprived of income is also to deprive them of dignity.

Whenever one feels like saying "the money that billionaire spent on his fleet of yachts could have been used better by the "public sector"", one should ask oneself when was the last time one heard of a billionaire buying an army of tanks and a set of nuclear weapons.

Where there is spontaneous inequality of wealth, there is relative poverty. Where there is spontaneous or enforced equality of wealth, there is absolute poverty. Thus, there can be no society without poverty, but only a spontaneously unequal one can successfully deal with its worst kind.

COMFORT, DISTRESS, HAPPINESS, AND TROUBLE

Achieving peace of mind is the dual process of maximizing self-awareness and minimizing self-consciousness.

Achieving peace of mind is the dual task of becoming aware of the extent of stupidity in the world and resolving not to contribute to it by refusing to dwell on it.

Bad may be less bad than worse, but that doesn't make it any better.

Fulfillment: the frame of mind in which success is neither a process nor an event, but a state of being.

Happiness: fulfillment without boredom.

Happiness is the ability to stay intrinsically motivated to exist.

Happiness is the state of letting go of all expectations while keeping the ability to wonder.

Happiness without liberty is no more possible than wisdom without knowledge.

If the best thing you can say about something is that it is a "necessary evil", then it is as obviously evil as it is unnecessary.

It takes a common thug to commit injustice, but it takes an exceptional thug to call it "social justice".

Liberty is to happiness what oxygen is to life.

Patience is the ability to enjoy the calm of boredom.

Peace of mind is skepticism without bitterness, detachment without apathy, comfort without pleasure, and focus without tension.

Peace of mind is the ability to maintain the intensity of feeling from an intellectual distance.

Perfection is the horizon of achievement.

Perseverance is the art of turning anxiety into excitement.

Suffering is to happiness what effort is to achievement.

Technology is to philosophy as the enjoyment of comfort is to the avoidance of apathy.

The best way to turn people into enemies is to convince them that they are entitled to one another's friendship.

The existence of unhappiness in the developed world does not show that material comfort is not a necessary condition of happiness, but that it is not a sufficient condition of it.

The first step in defeating evil is to stop believing in its necessity.

The first step on the road to success is to stop accepting subsidies for failure.

The key to mental comfort is getting rid of hopeful expectations while remaining open to pleasant surprises.

"The greater good" is the most common euphemism for the greatest evil.

The most potent source of misery is the belief in the right to happiness.

The psychological foundation of civilized life is the enjoyment of freedom for its own sake.

The ultimate achievement of an evildoer is to convince his victims that whatever good they happen to experience would be meaningless without all the evil they have to endure.

To accept an evil as necessary is not to follow one's reason, but to silence one's conscience.

To be a hero is not to die for one's country, but to live for one's world.

To claim that one can be happy without being free is to prove that one has no idea what happiness means.

AESTHETICS, CULTURE, AND TASTE

A commercial culture is a tautology. A political culture is an oxymoron.

A fool believes that a ban can eliminate debauchery. A person of reason knows that it can increase its attraction.

A fool believes that the way to destroy culture is to commercialize it. A person of reason knows that it is to subsidize it.

A libertarian boor is a possibility, but a statist gentleman is a contradiction.

A nationalist is someone who praises domestic illusions out of fear of confronting foreign realities.

Aesthetic maturity is the ability to deliberately ignore the fashionable without turning it into a fashion statement.

Aphorism: the precarious middle ground between brief banality and condensed obscurity.

Believing that the state can promote culture is like believing that putting a gun to someone's head is a gentleman's offer.

Border: the geographical expression of tribal parochialism.

Collectivism: the practice of exploiting humans in the name of humankind.

Conformity: intellectual suicide in slow motion.

Culture is liberty proud of its potential. Decadence is liberty ashamed of its misuse.

Culture is the aesthetic expression of the primacy of the individual.

Decadence is not a symptom of enjoying too much liberty, but of taking liberty for granted.

Ethics without aesthetics is preachiness. Aesthetics without ethics is decadence.

Fashion is to beauty what propaganda is to truth.

Individualism is to collectivism as society is to a herd.

Liberty is to culture what honesty is to character.

Nationalism: the curious idea that tribal prejudices are morally superior to universal values.

Political correctness: the notion that the ultimate argumentative skill is the ability to express outraged hysteria.

Social maturity consists not in accepting social customs, but in customizing social acceptance.

Subsidized culture is barbarism in denial.

The fact that libertarianism is not concerned with matters of culture does not make it weaker by virtue of cultural incompleteness, but stronger by virtue of cultural universality.

The most common sign of common sense and common decency is putting trust in liberty and abhorring violence.

The only guarantee of freedom of culture is a culture of freedom.

The world will know peace when the fiction of national interests is replaced by the reality of individual rights.

There are few things more tragicomically embarrassing than a would-be intellectual trying to flatter himself by wallowing in anecdotes about the idiocy of "rednecks".

Tradition: the emergency brake of unreflective progress.

Two unmistakable features of every barbaric society is distrust of the merchants and love of the military.

Vulgarity is to culture what cruelty is to morals.

KNOWLEDGE, EXPECTATIONS, ORDER, AND CHAOS

A civilized person uses reason to evaluate his instincts. A barbarian uses reason to justify his instincts.

A fool believes that uncertainty infects human life with the misery of fear. A person of reason knows that it imbues human life with the benefit of choice.

A little knowledge makes one believe that he knows everything. Some knowledge makes one afraid of how little he knows. A lot of knowledge makes one accept that he knows nothing.

A scientist believes that science is a source of knowledge. A pseudoscientist believes that science is the source of knowledge.

A seeming ontological nihilist believes that nothing really exists. A real ontological nihilist believes that nothing only seems to exist.

A successful prediction is a mental journey to the least impossible of the future worlds.

A technocrat is someone too dull to be an inventor, too technically inept to be a scientist, too reality-averse to be an entrepreneur, and too power-hungry to be a consultant.

A utopian believes in changing human nature. A realist believes in unleashing its potential.

A wise person is someone who is grateful for being called a fool when he's wrong, indifferent to being called a fool when he's right, embarrassed at being called a sage when he's right, and troubled by being called a sage when he's wrong.

All delusions aside, personal development consists in little more than scrubbing oneself clean of endless layers of folly.

An optimistic optimist hopes that the world won't end tomorrow. A pessimistic optimist fears that it may. An optimistic pessimist hopes that it will. A pessimistic pessimist fears that it won't.

As the world is increasingly filled with intellectuals, intelligence becomes increasingly less important than common sense.

Competence is the intelligent use of knowledge. Wisdom is the intelligent use of intelligence.

Developing practical wisdom is the process of extracting the timeless from the timely.

Education allows one to deal with ignorant superstition. Common sense allows one to deal with educated superstition.

Feeding one's mind on the diet of news is the surest path to mental indigestion.

Honest ignorance is wisdom compared to fake knowledge.

Ignorance is the absence of authentic knowledge. Stupidity is the presence of pretended knowledge.

Ignorance: the buffer against the torment of omniscience without omnipotence.

Imagination may be more important than knowledge, but imagination without knowledge is worse than knowledge without imagination.

In the land of educated idiots, the rationally ignorant is king.

In the pre-information age, erudition was knowing all there is to know. In the information age, erudition is knowing what there is to know.

In the pre-information age, generating knowledge consisted in breaking the silence. In the information age, it consists in cutting through the noise.

In the pre-information age, personal development consisted in a steady accumulation of rare common sense. In the information age, it consists in a steady resistance to ubiquitous nonsense.

Information is understood data. Knowledge is understood information. Wisdom is understood knowledge.

Innovating is the process of making scarce goods free. Copyrighting is the process of making free goods scarce.

Insight: a sudden tear in the veil of one's ignorance.

Intelligence allows for predicting the unknown. Wisdom allows for predicting the unknowable.

It is dangerous to underestimate the stupidity of the masses, but it is fatal to underestimate the stupidity of intellectuals.

It is possible
to copyright a haiku.
IP is a farce.

It takes a simpleton to do something plainly stupid, but it takes an intellectual to do something incomprehensibly stupid.

Knowledge is to wisdom as confidence is to serenity.

Modernity: artificial order.
Postmodernity: artificial chaos.
Post-postmodernity: spontaneous chaos.
Normality: spontaneous order.

Modernity: the quality of not yet having passed the test of time.

Moral wisdom acknowledges the fact that some evils may be inevitable. Moral stupidity concludes that they are therefore necessary.

Optimism cures the symptoms of disappointment. Pessimism cures its cause.

Philosophy begins with the impulse to chase after the infinite and ends with the realization that a finite chaser is not quite up to the task.

Philosophy is the most tortuous road from curiosity to confusion.

Positivism: the intellectual refuge of those too absent-minded to become serious natural scientists and too narrow-minded to become serious philosophers.

"Postmodernism" is to scholarship what decadence is to art.

"Postmodernism": the notion that the ultimate intellectual skill is the ability to produce arcane stupidity.

Propaganda: education made into a right.

"Public education" is the institutional foundation of mental totalitarianism.

"Public education" is to the mind what public flogging is to the body.

Saying "it is a good theory, but it wouldn't work in practice" is the most common sign that one has no idea whatever what a good theory is.

Science cannot eliminate metaphysics, but it can force it to level up.

Scientism is the only religion that sees hubris as a virtue.

Scientism is the only superstition that not only assures its followers that they are free of superstition, but that they are also immune to it.

Scientism is the romanticism of nerds.

Scientism: metaphysics in denial of metaphysics.

Stupidity is feeling comfortable with one's ignorance. Wisdom is not feeling uncomfortable with it.

Stupidity is ignorance of one's ignorance. Wisdom is knowledge of one's lack of knowledge.

Stupidity is the belief that you may know before thinking. Wisdom is the belief that you may not know after thinking.

Stupidity is the refusal to battle against one's ignorance. Wisdom is the ability to lose this battle with grace.

Technocratic do-gooders are the ultimate proof that there is no contradiction between intelligence and stupidity.

The adjective "social" added to a word turns it into its opposite, as in "service", "security", "work", "welfare", and "justice".

The difference between a confident man and a confidence man is that the former buys into his predictions, while the latter sells them out.

The difference between an intellectual and a person of reason is that they both doubt the wisdom of the masses, but the latter also doubts the wisdom of intellectuals.

The exclusive focus on "big news" is the exclusive province of small minds.

The fine line between moral wisdom and moral stupidity is the difference between realizing that evil is sometimes indistinguishable from good and believing that it makes the two identical.

The goal of technology is to determine what makes reality comfortable. The goal of philosophy is to determine what makes comfort real.

The greatest triumph of evil is to convince its victims of its own necessity.

The greatest value of experience is not that it offers us knowledge, but that it frees us from expectations.

The main benefit of interacting with intellectuals consists not in becoming appreciative of the power of the human intellect, but in becoming aware of its weakness.

The main epistemic virtue in the information age is selective ignorance.

The most effective way to make humanities degenerate into charlatanism is to try to make them "scientific".

The most flagrant symptom of intellectual decay is the trend to reject the "dogmatism" of logic.

The most important lesson of the information age is that wisdom consists as much of general knowledge as it does of particular ignorance.

The most sobering testimony to the rarity of genuine intelligence is not an encounter with a typical bumpkin, but an encounter with a typical intellectual.

The most useful knowledge comes from understanding the extent of one's ignorance. The most harmful ignorance comes from misconstruing the extent of one's knowledge.

The only good thing about technocrats is that they are far too dull to aspire to be "philosopher kings".

The ontology of logic in one sentence: a tautology is what it is, a paradox is what it is not, and everything else is something else.

To believe in the ownership of ideas is to believe in the enslavement of minds.

Trying to exchange arguments with a "postmodernist" is like trying to renovate a building with a vandal.

Uncertainty is the price we pay for existence.

When your mind is in the wrong place, it absolutely doesn't matter where your heart is.

Wisdom is an admission of stupidity that culminates a lifetime of searching for wisdom.

Wisdom is the ability to forgive stupidity while being relentless in fighting it.

Wisdom is the ability to make one's ignorance harmless.

Wisdom is the ability to simplify the complex without reducing it.

Wisdom is the skill of being passionate in one's understanding of reality, but dispassionate in one's judgment of it.

ABOUT THE AUTHOR

Jakub Bożydar Wiśniewski is a libertarian theorist and a researcher in the tradition of the Austrian School of Economics. He has been a fellow at the Institute for Humane Studies and at the Ludwig von Mises Institute. He has published peer-reviewed articles in philosophy, economics, and political economy in numerous scholarly journals.

www.ingramcontent.com/pod-product-compliance
Lightning Source LLC
Chambersburg PA
CBHW050519290526
45786CB00007B/2620